# INTRODUCTION

**The Edge Behind the Desk**

Hotels are supposed to be predictable.
Check in. Sleep. Check out.
That's the brochure version.
This book is about everything that happens between those steps.

For years, I worked the front desk, days, nights, weekends, holidays, and especially the hours when common sense clocks out and chaos checks in early. By the time midnight hits, the hotel stops being a business and starts being a filter. The rules soften. The city goes quiet. And the people who show up aren't always there for rooms.

Between midnight and 3:30 a.m., the desk becomes something else entirely.

A confessional.
A courtroom.
A daycare for adults.
A reality show with no cameras and no script.

Guests arrive tired, drunk, overconfident, entitled, heartbroken, lost, hiding, celebrating or all of the above. They bring their assumptions, their baggage, emotional and otherwise, and a firm belief that this situation is somehow different and the rules shouldn't apply to them. Standing between them and whatever they want is a front desk agent armed with a computer, a policy manual, and the faint hope that tonight will be quiet.

## INTRODUCTION

It never is.

*Before going further, something needs to be made clear. What you're about to read reflects my personal experience and perspective working the front desk. It is not a statement of policy. It is not a judgment on how anyone chooses to live their life. And it does not speak for anyone else. It is simply what I have experienced doing the job.*

When you work the front desk, you meet people from everywhere, every country, every background, every walk of life. Some good. Some difficult. Men. Women. Over time, the range of presentations has expanded. The desk puts you in a very specific position: you are expected to be professional, neutral, and efficient, regardless of what is happening internally.

That skill took me years to learn.

Early in my career, my face showed exactly what I was thinking. Eventually, you learn how not to react, not because you agree, not because you approve, but because the job requires neutrality. Language matters at the desk. Sir. Ma'am. Good afternoon. Those words used to be automatic. Now, sometimes, they aren't.

When there's uncertainty, you default to neutral professionalism. Not debate. Not validation. Not analysis.

"Good afternoon. How may I help you?"

That's it.

The job isn't to resolve identity questions or internal frameworks. The job is to check people in accurately, protect their privacy, enforce policy, and keep things moving. Assumptions get you in trouble fast. Names repeat. Couples don't match expectations. Mistakes happen, not out of malice, but because humans are processing information quickly under pressure.

## INTRODUCTION

Front desk work teaches one lesson early:
Assume nothing.
React only to what's confirmed.
Stay neutral.

But neutrality alone doesn't get you through the night.

There's another skill I don't talk about often.

It didn't come from hospitality training.
It didn't come from customer service manuals.
It came from incarceration.

Good or bad, that period of my life taught me one thing very clearly: I fear no man.

That doesn't mean intimidation. It doesn't mean posturing or provocation. If you're truly strong, you don't pick on the weak. But incarceration is a jungle, and in that environment you either develop awareness, presence, and resolve, or you become prey. You learn to stand your ground quietly.

When you leave that world and re-enter normal life, something changes. You still see people. You still deal with conflict. But you no longer see anyone you're supposed to be afraid of.

That edge followed me into night audit.

Between midnight and 3:30 a.m., hotels attract everything the rest of society has finished dealing with for the day. I'll say this plainly: I do not believe women should work night audit alone. That isn't disrespect, it's experience. It's not about capability. I've worked with excellent female auditors, and many hotels assign security for that reason. But the reality is simple: too many robberies, too many incidents, too many stories I've personally witnessed or heard. One bad encounter out of ten is still one too many.

## INTRODUCTION

In more than ten years working night audit across multiple properties, I have never been robbed. Never been attempted. That isn't luck. That's presence.

At one in the morning, I've already seen you on camera before you reach the desk. I'm already reading posture, pace, intent. When I step out and greet you, there's an unspoken understanding, man to man. Nothing aggressive. Nothing verbal. Just clarity.

"What's up?"

That's usually enough.

Most encounters end exactly how they should. Directions given. Bathroom located. Keys issued. I return to the desk, watch the cameras, do my job. That edge isn't about intimidation, it's about boundaries. Common-sense boundaries.

You don't wander into environments you don't understand and test them. Strength isn't recklessness. It's judgment.

The stories in this book are snapshots from behind the counter, short encounters, unfiltered moments, real consequences. They aren't exaggerated. They aren't polished. They aren't cleaned up for corporate comfort. They're funny because they're absurd. They're absurd because they happened. And they happened more often than most people would ever believe.

If you've worked in hospitality, you'll recognize these moments immediately. If you haven't, you may never look at a hotel, or the person behind the desk, the same way again.

Welcome to the other side of the counter.

**No vacancy for common sense.**

NO VACANCY FOR COMMON SENSE

GARY HAYWOOD

# NO VACANCY FOR COMMON SENSE

# CHAPTER 1

## The Gatekeepers

This isn't really a story. It's a reminder. Respect the front desk. People don't realize this, but front desk agents are gatekeepers. We are the final authority between you and your room. We don't just hand out keys, we decide whether you get one at all. Ninety-nine percent of the time, everything goes smoothly. You walk up. I greet you. You show your ID. You sign the registration card. I tell you about breakfast, the pool, the Wi-Fi. You get your key. You're on your way.

That's how it's supposed to work. But then there's the one percent. The people who think the front desk is a punching bag. The ones who talk down to you, belittle you, swear at you, or treat you like you're beneath them, *and then* expect you to help them. Let me be clear: I try not to take things personally. You don't know what someone's going through. Someone could have lost a job, a spouse, a child. People carry heavy things, and I get that. But here's what I also know: I am a professional. And my job is to check you in, not to be your emotional landfill.

Customer service means patience. It means dealing with irritation, frustration, bad moods. That's expected. What is *not* expected is being yelled at, demeaned, or disrespected and then asked for a room key like nothing happened. That's not how this works. At a certain point, the situation passes the point of no return. And when that happens, the tone changes.

"Sir, I don't believe our hotel is a good fit for you."
"I'm going to cancel your reservation."
"You'll receive a full refund."
"There are other hotels in the area."

Nothing sobers someone up faster than that sentence. Because suddenly the reality hits: the power isn't with the guest, it's with the person behind the desk. You cannot get a key without our approval. You cannot stay without our consent. It's quiet power. Background power. But it's real. I've canceled reservations. More than one. I've asked guests to leave. I've had to call the police when they refused, because they always refuse.

"You can't do that."
"You don't have that right."
"I want your manager."
　No.
No.
And no.
　Even if I could call my manager, I wouldn't. This situation doesn't warrant it. And they *hate* that answer but it's the truth. I give people chances. Plenty of them. I'll step away from the desk. I'll suggest taking a moment to breathe. I'll offer a reset.
　"Let's take a minute and try again."

Because who *wants* to cancel a reservation? But make no mistake, if you continue to act a fool, I will excuse you. Calmly. Professionally. Without hesitation. Because no room, no rate, no reservation is worth being disrespected.

Hotels are not lawless zones.

Front desk agents are not powerless.

And courtesy isn't optional, it's required.

Respect the gatekeepers. Or find another gate.

GARY HAYWOOD

## Room Service: Three Early Lessons

Early in my hotel career, I worked room service. Back then, early to mid-2000s, room service was a real department. Not like now. In Vegas, four-star, five-diamond properties. This is where people made money. Good tips. Simple rules. Be polite. Get the food there hot. Get the signature. Leave.

There was actually a sign over the doorway that said something like: *Get the signature. Don't look around. Leave.* Very clear. Very intentional. Because room service puts you directly inside someone else's private space.

**So my first delivery.** Lunch. Hamburger. Middle of the day. I knock on the door. It opens. And immediately...
this is an adult film shoot. The woman who opens the door is topless, in her underwear, smiling like she's been waiting all day. I'm young. I'm new. And my brain completely short-circuits.

All I'm thinking is: *What the hell is happening right now.*

She looks back into the room and says,
"Lunch is here."

The actors stop what they're doing, grab towels, cover up just enough, and walk over. One of them doesn't bother covering up at all. Meanwhile, I'm doing everything in my power to look *only at faces.* I present the food. I ask, politely, for the signature. They can see I'm embarrassed. They're laughing. Not in a mean way, just amused. Someone pats me on the shoulder.
"Thanks for the food."

They tip me forty dollars. That was my first room-service tip. I go back downstairs. My boss asks,
"How was it?"

I tell him. He smiles and says,
"Yeah. I know. That's why I sent you."

Lesson learned.

**Another delivery.**

Dinner. I knock on the door. A woman calls out, "I'm in here."

I walk in. There's an older woman, naked, strapped to the bed, blindfolded, spread out.

The tray paperwork, already signed, is resting on her chest. I don't ask questions. I place the food down.

Carefully. Gently retrieve the signed slip. And leave. Door closed. Back downstairs, my boss asks how it went. I tell him. He pauses and says, "That's... different."

Then he asks the only question that matters:

"You got the signature?"

"Yes."

"All right. Good."


**Final Delivery**

A convention weekend.

They order a large lunch, fries, sandwiches, clearly for multiple people. I knock. The door opens.

And I'm face-to-face with what looks like Yogi Bear. Full costume. Behind him, more costumes. Dog suits. A woman dressed as a poodle.

It's hot in the room. Very hot. I do not inspect. I do not judge. I do not linger.

Room service rules apply. Here's your food. May I have the signature, please? That's it.

I've also delivered to rooms where people were clearly high. Disoriented. Out of it. But that's part of hotel work. They rented the room. They have privacy. What they do inside it is their business. Room service was profitable.

But more than that, it was eye-opening. You learn quickly how to focus. How to stay professional. How to follow procedure no matter what's happening around you.

Get the signature.

Don't look around.

Leave.

Those rules existed for a reason.

## The Fire Alarm

There is never a good time for a fire alarm to go off in a hotel. Never.

It doesn't matter if it's two in the afternoon or two in the morning. It doesn't matter if it's July or if it's ten degrees below zero in February. A fire alarm is never helpful, never convenient, and almost never what it claims to be.

In my experience, it's usually popcorn. Or toast. Or someone who decided that cooking was a good idea at 1:47 a.m.

Here's how it works.

The alarm doesn't ease into the situation. It doesn't give you a warning or a courtesy beep. It detonates. Sirens screaming, lights flashing, the entire building announcing to the world that something has gone very wrong. And depending on the type of hotel, all it takes is one guest opening a front door or a stairwell door at the wrong moment for the entire system to lose its mind.

When the alarm goes off, everything stops. Doesn't matter what you're doing. Doesn't matter where you are. Doesn't matter how warm your room was five seconds ago.

Everyone. Gets. Out.

Guests pour into the lobby wrapped in towels, pajamas, blankets, winter coats thrown over bare feet. Kids crying. Dogs barking. Phones recording. Faces already angry before they even know who to blame.

And somehow, without fail, that person is me.

I'm the front desk clerk. Which means, in the court of public opinion, I personally pulled the fire alarm. I personally ruined your sleep. I personally chose this exact moment for you to stand outside in sub-zero weather questioning every life decision that brought you here.

As the alarm screams, the phone rings.

Of course it does.

"Front desk."

"Yeah, there's an alarm going off. Should I be worried?"

What I am thinking: "No. Not at all. The smoke, the lights, the sirens, *that's just ambiance*. Please, by all means, stay in your room. Take a nap. I'll call you back if the building explodes".

What I want to say is:

"It's a fire alarm. Get out. Why are you calling me?"

What I have to say is:

"Yes, sir, please exit the building immediately."

Meanwhile, I'm not even supposed to be at the front desk anymore. Policy says I should evacuate too. But there I am, standing behind the counter like a hotel gargoyle, apologizing while the building screams and the fire department makes their way over, because they have to. They always have to. The system won't shut off until they personally arrive, flip the switch, and charge the hotel a fine for the privilege. By the time it's over, it's exactly what it always is.

A false alarm.

Ninety-nine percent of the time. Burnt popcorn. Overcooked food. Someone who "was just heating something up."

Guests file back inside slowly, silently, staring daggers straight through me. I apologize. Over and over. Like I did this on purpose.

"I'm sorry about that."

"False alarm."

"Sorry for the inconvenience."

"Please come back inside and stay warm."

I say it until the words stop meaning anything. The first fire alarm of your hotel career scares the hell out of you. Your heart races. Your brain jumps to worst-case scenarios. Especially on night audit, when you're the only one in the building. No staff. No backup. Just you, the alarm, and the realization that if something is actually wrong, this just became very real.

Eventually, though, you learn. You learn the sound. You learn the routine. You learn the looks.

Every front desk worker has lived this story. Different hotels. Same chaos. Same blame. Same apology.

And it's never,

ever,

the right time.

## The Third-Party Trap (Prepaid Reservations)

If there is one thing guaranteed to ruin a perfectly normal hotel check-in, it's a third-party reservation. Expedia. Booking.com. Agoda. Insert middleman here.

People use them for one reason and one reason only: to save money. Ten percent. Fifteen percent. Maybe twenty if the stars align. And on paper, it looks great.

In reality, it's a headache and a half. Here's how it usually starts.

A guest walks up to the front desk already irritated. Not confused, *irritated*. They announce, confidently,

"I have a reservation."

I ask for their name. I search the system. Nothing.

That's when the phone comes out. They shove it in my face like it's a badge. Bank statement. Confirmation email. Screenshot. Highlighted. Circled. Annotated like evidence in a courtroom.

"See? Right there."

Yes, I see it.

What I don't see is *you,* in *my* system.

And that's the part no one understands.

I don't check people in based on screenshots.

I don't check people in based on bank charges.

I don't check people in because an app says you're supposed to exist. I check you in when the reservation is actually populated in the hotel system by the third party. Until that happens, you're a ghost. And explaining that to people is like explaining gravity to a goldfish.

"But I made the reservation!"

Yes, but not with us.

"So what does that mean?"

It means you have to call them. That's when the meltdown starts.

"What do you mean *call them*? I'm standing right here!"

Right. And I'm standing right here too, unable to do a damn thing until *they* fix *their* mistake. This is the moment where I realize that a shocking number of adults have no idea how email works.

Or receipts.

Or confirmations.

Or the fact that when you click *I agree on terms and conditions*, you've actually agreed to something.

I politely explain, slowly, that when you book a third-party reservation, you enter your credit card, click through the disclaimers, provide an email address, and receive a confirmation. That confirmation contains a phone number. That phone number connects you to the people who actually control your reservation.

They stare at me like I just invented fire.

The non-refundable ones. The words are right there. Bold. Clear. Impossible to miss.

**NON-REFUNDABLE.**

Once you book it, that money is gone. No cancellations. No changes. No exceptions. And yet, without fail, they call.

"My plans changed."

"My kid got sick."

"My flight was canceled."

"My dog ate my passport."

"My cousin's neighbor's uncle had an emergency."

They plead. They negotiate. They beg. Then they call the third party. The third party reads from a script. Then the third party calls us.

"Our mutual guest is requesting a refund."

And I respond like a lawyer who's said this a thousand times.

"What do the terms and conditions say?"

Silence.

"Those are the terms the guest agreed to."

"Well... can you make an exception?"

No. I cannot. And even if I could, I wouldn't. Because the moment you make one exception, the entire system collapses.

The best part? The customer service. Outsourced. One hundred and fifty percent. Scripted. Polite to the point of useless. They're not in the U.S. They don't understand the hotel. They don't understand the situation. They're just reading lines and passing the problem along. Meanwhile, the guest is standing in front of me, angry, tired, and convinced I personally created third-party reservations just to ruin their trip.

**So here's the truth, straight from the front desk:**

If you want control, book direct.

If you want flexibility, book direct.

If you want fewer headaches, book direct.

Pay the extra ten or fifteen percent.

Save yourself the stress. Save the front desk the stress. Stop picking up pennies in front of a bulldozer.

Because third-party reservations don't save you money.

They just delay the pain.

# CHAPTER 4

## What the Front Desk Sees

This isn't one story. It's a cumulative reality. Five-star hotels. One-star hotels. Everything in between. Years behind a front desk teaches you one thing very quickly:

You see **everything,** whether you want to or not. Internally, I've watched coworkers sleep with coworkers. Staff with supervisors. Supervisors with staff. Human nature. Not my business. I don't judge it, and I don't participate in it.

I'm front desk. I mind my business. I have my own wife. I've been married over a decade. I don't need drama, complications, or whispered conversations. Don't tell me anything. Don't ask me anything. I know nothing. That mindset is survival.

Over the years, I've watched couples arrive together and couples arrive pretending they aren't couples. Husbands. Wives. Affairs disguised as "late check-ins." It's always the same patterns, and after enough time, you don't even need to try to notice them. You just do.

**One night stands out.**

I was working night audit at the Westford Regency Inn and Conference Center. It had to be around 2:00 a.m. A woman walked up to the front desk. Calm. Polite. Direct. She knew exactly where she was and why she was there. She looked at me and said without hesitation:

"I'm here to kill my husband."

No raised voice. No drama. Just matter-of-fact.

I responded the only way a night auditor can: neutral, professional, steady. She didn't need to tell me his name. She already knew it. She knew he was there. She said she'd wait in the lobby. The lobby was large. There were tall planters, five feet high, with thick plants. Enough to sit quietly, partially obscured.

She waited.

Not long after, her husband came downstairs with the woman he had checked in with. Laughing. Relaxed. Comfortable. Walking through the lobby like nothing in the world could touch him.

Then his wife stood up. She said his name.

That moment, that split second, is burned into my memory. The shock. The realization. The immediate collapse of whatever fantasy he was living in.

It wasn't pretty. It never is.

They left. That's where my involvement ended. That's always where my involvement ends. Because the front desk isn't a confessional. People forget that.

Over the years, they come up asking questions:
"Is so-and-so staying here?"
"Can you tell me what room he's in?"
"I just need to know if she checked in."

No. We can't. We won't. It's illegal. Guest privacy is absolute unless permission is explicitly given. Hotels don't bend on that, not because we're protecting your secret, but because lawsuits don't care about your relationship problems. That said, when you work full-time, you recognize patterns. Cash payments. One name checking in while the other waits quietly behind. No luggage. Late arrivals. Debit cards that aren't in the guest's name. Attempts to avoid paper trails.

There is **always** a trail.

People think hotels are invisible spaces. They're not. Everything is logged. Everything leaves a record. Even when you pay cash, something ties you to that room.

I don't judge any of it.

I don't care.

Until it affects my shift.

If someone starts screaming in the hallway at 2:30 a.m., that's now my problem. If a spouse shows up furious, that's now my problem. If a man wants to fight, it's always physical, and that's now my problem.

Women usually confront. Men usually escalate. It's never calm. It's never civilized. And it's never worth it.

That's the part people don't see.

Hotels aren't romantic backdrops.

They're pressure chambers.

And the front desk is where consequences eventually pass through, whether quietly, or all at once.

# CHAPTER 5

# Room Service for Chaos

For whatever reason, drugs and hotels go together like ice and bad decisions. I don't know why. Maybe it's the anonymity. Maybe it's the idea that you're away from home, away from responsibility, away from people who know you. You check in, shut the door, and suddenly you're in a bubble where consequences feel optional.

Fine.

You're over twenty-one. You paid for the room. Do your thing.

The problem starts when the drugs decide it's time to socialize. For reasons I will never understand, people who are completely out of their minds always seem to think the *front desk* is the place to process it.

Not their room.

Not quietly.

Not privately.

No, they come down to me, twitching, sweating, vibrating like a phone on silent, ready to explain something that makes absolutely no sense.

I've had guests convinced they could fly and wanted advice on which window to use.

Guests asking if I had seen the Martians who just landed in their room.

Guests wandering the hallways naked like it was perfectly reasonable behavior.

I've seen the full catalog.

Meth, especially, is always... memorable. Those guests can't stand still. Can't finish a sentence. Can't stop moving their hands, their jaw, their entire body. They'll try to have a serious conversation with you while doing a full-body jazz routine, eyes wide, confidence high, logic gone. They really try, though. I'll give them that. They work *hard* to sound normal.

They don't succeed.

Watching them is like watching Pinocchio on a bad day, too much movement, too much confidence, and absolutely no connection to reality. And there I am, nodding politely, thinking:

Should you even be outside right now?

Should I be calling the police?

Should I walk you back to your room?

Will you listen to me?

Are you going to snap and punch me?

All of those thoughts run through your head in about three seconds.

Most of the time, I choose the silent prayer option. Please go back to your room. Please crawl under a rock. Please not on my shift.

Every front desk worker knows that feeling.

You clock in and the first thing you ask isn't "How's occupancy?" It's: Who's crazy? What room is a problem? Who's on something?

Housekeeping always knows first. They see the rooms. They see what's left behind. They see the damage, the filth, the evidence of someone treating a hotel room like a disposable universe.

Sometimes, though, it's invisible. Some people are high and happy. You'd never know. They smile, go about their business, don't bother anyone. Those are the easy ones.

The hard ones are the ODs.

Those are the calls you never want. The sirens you don't forget. The moments when the job stops being funny and becomes very real, very fast.

You don't want medical examiners walking through your lobby.

You don't want to explain to police.

You don't want to think about how someone checked in and never checked out.

Back in the late '90s and early 2000s, the holidays made it worse.

People alone.

People spiraling.

People jumping from windows or making decisions they couldn't take back.

Hotels saw it all—quietly, behind the scenes, while everyone else slept. That's the part guests never see. Hotels aren't just places people rest. They're places people unravel.

And the front desk is where it all eventually shows up.

Right on cue.

## Executive Privilege

This happened at the Westford Regency Inn and Conference Center in between 2014 and 2022. Unlike some of the other places I'd worked, this was a full-service property. Banquets. Weddings. Conferences. Restaurant. Bar. Corporate money. Real money. The kind of place where deals get closed and egos get fed.

I worked night audit.

Which means I always showed up right when the party was winding down, or unraveling. One night, there was a business conference in-house. Big group. Big tabs. Big energy. I clock in, do my usual walk-through. I stop by the bar, say hello to the bartender, let everyone know night audit is on duty. Standard routine. I hadn't even made it back to the front desk yet when I heard it.

That sound.

The unmistakable, violent sound of someone losing a battle they should have quit an hour ago. I turn the corner, and there he is.

An older gentleman. Immaculately dressed. White shirt. Jacket. Corporate polished. On his hands and knees. Vomiting all over the marble floor like it was part of the evening's entertainment. And the first thing that goes through my head isn't sympathy.

It's: *Who the hell is cleaning that up?*

Because it's not me.

I'm front desk.

I'm not maintenance.

I'm definitely not housekeeping. And it's third shift, there's no one else around. So I do what any seasoned hotel employee would do. I turn around and pretend I didn't see a thing. I go back behind the desk and mind my business.

A little while later, a woman approaches the front desk.

Calm.

Professional.

Polite.

She asks for a mop and some towels. Says she has "something to take care of."

I give them to her without asking questions. And to her credit, she does an incredible job.

Cleans the entire mess.

Marble floor spotless.

No drama.

No complaints.

Returns the mop bucket and towels like this is a normal Tuesday. That's when curiosity gets the better of me. I pull her aside.

"So," I ask, "what the hell was that?"

She sighs, casually.

"That's my boss."

Your boss?

"Yeah," she says. "He just closed a half-million-dollar deal. He was celebrating. Drank too much."

I blink.

"He's in his seventies," she adds.

And you cleaned it up?

"I'm his executive assistant," she says, like that explains everything.

Executive assistant.

Right.

She returns to the party like nothing happened. Like she didn't just mop corporate success off the floor five minutes ago. And I stand there thinking about it.

This man closed a half-million-dollar deal.

Probably gave a speech.

Probably shook hands.

Probably toasted to success.

Then decided the best way to celebrate was to get on his hands and knees and vomit in a hotel hallway, while his assistant quietly cleaned it up behind him.

Hotels will teach you a lot. One of the biggest lessons? Titles don't make you dignified. Money doesn't make you graceful. And success doesn't stop you from embarrassing yourself in public.

It just means someone else cleans it up.

# CHAPTER 7

# The Pool, the French, and the Limits of My Maturity

Over the years, I've checked in people from everywhere.
**EVERYWHERE.**
Tanzania.
Australia.
Uganda.
Afghanistan.
Nepal.
China.
South Korea.
Islands most people couldn't find on a map.

I've watched passports hit the desk like postcards from the entire planet. Most people are fine. Normal. Predictable. You check in, you go to your room, you sleep, you leave.

But then there's the French. Now, let me be clear, I like French food. I studied French in school. I wasn't great at it, but I tried. I have no problem with France as a concept.

But when it comes to **hotel pools**, I do not understand the French at all. At multiple hotels, we had indoor pools. Heated. Enclosed. With signage. Rules. The universal, unspoken understanding that *this is a public space.*

For whatever reason, the French treat this like a suggestion.

They love being naked.

Now listen, do what you want in your room. Your house. Your private villa. Somewhere in Europe where this is apparently normal. But a public hotel pool?

No. Absolutely not. I did not sign up for that.

And it's never the young ones. It's always someone in their fifties or older. Confident. Unbothered. Just strolling around like nudity is part of the amenities package.

I've had French guests swim naked.

Lounge naked.

Walk from the pool to the spa naked.

And yes, *get locked out of their room naked.*

One guy comes down to the front desk in his skivvies like this is a casual inconvenience.

"Oui... I am locked out."

Sir. This is a lobby.

And it's not just the French. Let's be honest. Hotels attract a special category of behavior. People show up half-dressed. Naked. Drunk. Wrapped in towels that are barely holding on. They lean over the counter. They breathe too close. They talk like personal space is a myth.

And you stand there, trained, professional, trying not to let your face say what your brain is screaming. Because as an adult, you're expected to be mature. And as a hotel employee, you're expected to act like none of this is strange.

But it is strange.

## NO VACANCY FOR COMMON SENSE

It's strange that I have to explain clothing to grown adults.
It's strange that public spaces need reminders.
It's strange how many people lose all common sense the moment they check into a hotel.

Hotels strip people down, not just physically, apparently, but mentally.
Rules feel optional.
Decorum feels negotiable.
Accountability checks out early.
And I just stand there, behind the desk, watching humanity parade past me in towels, underwear, and bad decisions, wondering how we've made it this far as a species.

Welcome to hospitality.

Please keep your clothes on.

## CHAPTER 8

# The Gym Shortcut

This story took place at the Westford Regency. I worked there from 2014 to 2024, about ten years. It was a five-star, full-service hotel. Banquets, weddings, indoor pool, indoor hot tub. A massive fitness facility downstairs—around 2,200 square feet—with a sauna, racquetball court, yoga room, cycling room. On paper, it was impressive.

In reality, it was stuck in the 1980s. Nice bones. Old systems. Constant problems. Leaks. Breakdowns. Deferred updates. Over time, it became obvious the hotel was a financial black hole. The owner was a multimillionaire and didn't care. It was a tax write-off. Once you work somewhere long enough, you can tell. My gripe here isn't management or money.

It's the gym.

That gym was unavoidable. I didn't go there to work out, I went there because something was always broken.

Sauna issue.

Locker issue.

Ceiling leak.

Or because it was the only shortcut to the laundry room on the other side of the building.

And every single time I walked through, I regretted it. Why?

Because grown men, completely naked, apparently felt compelled to start conversations with me.

Open showers, fine.

It's a locker room. Nudity comes with the territory. I get it.

But why are you talking to me?

I'm clearly just passing through. In and out. Maintenance brain on. And yet, full-blown conversations. No towel. No awareness. Just standing there like this is a networking event. Put a towel on. Or don't talk to me. That was easily the worst part of that gym. The rest of it wasn't much better.

You had the lifters grunting like they were pulling a car out of a ditch. If you're making that much noise, the weight is too heavy. Then came the mirror people, checking form, fine. That's normal.

But once phones became a thing?

Forget it.

Now nobody's working out. Everyone's modeling. Filming. Posing. Adjusting angles. Recording sets that never seem to end.

Are you here to exercise, or audition?

And then there were the talkers. Mid-set conversations. Eye contact. Nods. Like I'm part of the workout routine.

I'm not.

I'm just trying to get to the laundry room without seeing more than I need to see. Eventually, I learned to move fast. Head forward. Minimal acknowledgment. Get in, get out. Still, every time I had to cut through that gym, I knew exactly what I was walking into.

That place taught me a lot over ten years.

Mostly this:

Some people don't understand boundaries, even when they're completely naked and you're clearly just trying to do your job.

# CHAPTER 9

## When Law Enforcement Shows Up

If you work a hotel front desk long enough, you will interact with law enforcement. Police, state troopers, fire department, federal agencies, it's inevitable. Especially on second shift and overnight, the front desk becomes the point of contact.

By 2025, my interactions with ICE and Homeland Security increased significantly. Boston is a sanctuary city. Massachusetts is a sanctuary state. That reality shapes how law enforcement operates, and how hotels are expected to operate within that environment.

Hotels are private property. That matters.

Law enforcement officers do not have automatic access to guest information, occupancy details, or room locations. Without consent, exigent circumstances, or a warrant, that information is protected. As front desk staff, we are trained to cooperate with law enforcement but cooperation does not mean voluntary disclosure of protected guest information.

There's an important distinction there.

Most of the time, cooperation is mutual and professional. Officers respond to disturbances, welfare checks, or guests who refuse to vacate rooms after checkout. In those cases, their presence is welcome. We call them because we need them.

But not every situation is that simple.

There are times when guests explicitly request privacy for safety reasons. Domestic violence situations are a common example. A guest informs the front desk that they are trying to disappear. Management documents it. Front desk staff is instructed clearly: if anyone calls or asks for that guest by name, the response is simple, *they are not registered here.*

That is standard hotel procedure.

So when an officer walks in and asks, "I'm looking for Jane Doe," the answer is:

"No one by that name is staying here."

If pressed, the response remains the same.

"You're obstructing an investigation," is sometimes implied or directly stated.

The answer does not change.

"Officer, you're free to pursue your investigation. If you need anything further, feel free to obtain the appropriate paperwork. I'll be right here."

Most officers understand that. Some don't like it but understanding and liking are not the same thing.

Roughly 85–90% of interactions with law enforcement are professional and uneventful. You want that relationship to work. Hotels rely on police assistance regularly.

But the sanctuary framework complicates removals.

More than once in recent years, officers told us they were *not permitted* to forcibly remove certain individuals, even after checkout, particularly when immigration status was involved. We could ask politely. That was it.

Which creates a strange dynamic.

You're standing at a front desk, being told by someone with a badge and a firearm that they can't remove a trespassing guest, but you, the hotel employee, are still responsible for the situation.

It's frustrating. Deeply frustrating.

Still, this is why professionalism matters.

You learn quickly that how you speak to officers matters. Politeness matters. Respect matters. These are people who spend their shifts dealing with conflict, danger, and stupidity for hours at a time. They rarely get appreciation.

So I always thanked them.

Not "thank you for your service" in a ceremonial way, but "thank you for doing a job I wouldn't want to do." That matters. They notice it.

At the front desk, you're not just checking people in. You're navigating private property, public authority, guest safety, and legal boundaries, all at once.

And if you don't know where those lines are, you'll learn the hard way.

## CHAPTER 10

# A Star and a Half in a Five-Star Town

Lexington, Massachusetts is a high-end town.

Tree-lined streets. Multi-million-dollar homes. Old money quiet. The kind of place where people complain if the wrong color mailbox shows up.

The hotel I worked at was not that.

Out of five stars, this place was maybe a star and a half on a good day. It was a smoking hotel. It had cockroaches. It had bedbugs. The pool was green more often than it was blue and grew more mold than chlorine. It was the kind of hotel you didn't stay at, you *ended up* at.

But I needed the money.

Ten dollars an hour.

Night audit.

3rd Shift.

It paid the bills, so I worked there.

The layout was strange. The front desk was inside a main building, but the rooms were in separate exterior buildings. To get to your room, you had to leave the front desk, walk outside, and enter another building. Doors were supposed to stay locked.

One night, just another average night audit, I check in a guest. He goes to his room. A few minutes later, the phone rings.

"Hey," he says. "There's a man sleeping on the steps in my building."

That's not supposed to happen.

"How did he get in?" I ask. "The door should be locked."

"I don't know," he says. "But he's there."

Great.

So I grab my jacket and head over. Sitting on the steps is a guy, clearly homeless, clearly not a guest.

"Hey, man," I say. "You can't be here. You're going to have to leave."

He looks up at me and immediately says, "I got robbed."

That's not what you want to hear.

"Okay," I say. "If you got robbed, we need to call the police."

He loses it.

"Call the cops? Are you crazy? Someone's going to jail!"

Yes. That's usually how that works.

I take one look at him and know exactly what this is. Homeless. Looking for somewhere warm. Looking for somewhere quiet. Unfortunately, this isn't it.

"You can't stay here," I tell him. "You'll have to go to a shelter or somewhere else."

"No, man, I got robbed!"

Now I'm curious.

"All right," I say. "Before I call the police, let's get the story straight. They're going to ask questions."

"I don't want to talk to you," he snaps. "I want to talk to the cops."

Fine.

I bring him back to the front desk and call Lexington PD.

"Hi, this is the front desk," I say. "I have a gentleman here who says he's been robbed. A guest reported him sleeping in a stairwell. He asked me to call the police."

They say they'll send someone.

About fifteen minutes later, Officer O'Malley walks in. I knew him, night auditors tend to know the overnight cops. He looks at me.

"What's going on, Gary?"

I explain.

Another officer joins him, and they start asking the guy questions.

Where were you robbed?

Up the street.

Where exactly?

In a ditch.

In a ditch.

Okay.

Do you have ID?

No.

Where is it?

They took it.

Who took it?

Some guys.

Which guys?

I don't know.

The story is unraveling fast. It reminds me of those stories that sound believable until you hear them out loud, like they collapse under their own weight.

Then he gets angry.

"You don't believe me because I'm Black!"

Nope. This is where I quietly disengage.

I walk behind the counter and pretend to be very busy with absolutely nothing. I am not getting dragged into this.

The officers try to calm him down. He escalates. Raises his voice. Starts pacing.

Then, because there's always a moment when things cross from stupid to irreversible, he lunges at one of the cops.

That's it.

They take him down. Cuffs. Arrest. Gone.

The lobby goes quiet again.

And I'm left standing there thinking the same thing I've thought a thousand times working hotels:

People will say the dumbest things.

People will do the dumbest things.

And they will do them with absolute confidence.

No matter how long you work at a hotel, you are never surprised.

You just get better at stepping out of the way.

## CHAPTER 11

# MDMA at the Buckminster (2011)

I was working night audit at the Hotel Buckminster in Kenmore Square when the Bruins won the Stanley Cup in 2011.

If you weren't in Boston that night, it's hard to explain what the city turned into. It wasn't celebration, it was release. Streets flooded with people. Sirens everywhere. Police stacked shoulder to shoulder along Commonwealth Avenue. The air felt charged, like something could tip at any second.

And there I was, clocking in at 11:00 p.m.

Night audit runs from eleven at night to seven in the morning. You don't get the parade. You get the aftermath. You see who can't go home. Who shouldn't be out. Who is celebrating too hard, too long, and too chemically.

Earlier that evening, a guy from New Zealand checked in. Nice enough. He had one of the best rooms in the building, overlooking Kenmore Square. Around midnight, the phone rings.

"Hey, man... there are cops outside."

"Yeah," I tell him. "We're on Commonwealth Ave. That's normal."

Pause.

"They're not here for me, right?"

"No," I say. "They're not here for you."

He hangs up.

About thirty minutes later, the phone rings again.

"Hey… can you come up to my room?"

That's never a sentence you want to hear when you're alone on night audit. But I go. I knock. He cracks the door and peeks out, eyes wide, jittery.

"You sure they're not looking for me?"

I reassure him again.

Then he says, "You wanna come in?"

I shouldn't have, but I did.

Inside the room is exactly what you'd expect from a long Bruins night. One guy passed out in a chair. Another sprawled on the bed. Money on the table. White powder I don't ask about. A bowl of weed. The smell of celebration mixed with bad judgment.

He's talking fast. Friendly. Paranoid. Telling me about New Zealand. About the cops. Asking if I smoke weed. I respond:

"I do."

So we stand near the window, smoking, half-watching the celebration like two idiots pretending we're discreet.

Then, casually, like he's offering gum, he asks:

"You ever try MDMA?"

He pulls out a tiny bag, crystals. I've never seen it before. I'm in my early thirties and somehow I've never touched anything harder than weed.

"No," I say. "I don't do coke or hard drugs."

"No, no," he says. "This isn't like that. It's just an upper. Look it up."

I tell him I'm working. I need to be functional.

"You'll be functional," he says, confidently, like that means anything.

I hesitate.

Then I say yes.

He gives me a small amount. Free. Along with some weed. Tells me if I see cops coming upstairs, to give him a heads-up.

I taste it. It's awful. Bitter. Chemical. Instantly regrettable.

"How much do I need?"

"That's enough," he says.

I go back downstairs.

Nothing happens.

An hour passes. It's around 1:00 a.m.

Then my hands start sweating, beads, not normal sweat. My heart speeds up. Sitting still feels impossible. I need to move.

So I move.

I step outside. The cold air feels incredible. The noise feels alive. The city feels electric. I pace. I walk. I take the stairs, seven flights, marble floors, up and down like I'm training for something that doesn't exist.

I feel amazing.

Too amazing.

Back at the desk, it hits me: I'm high. Very high. I can't stop moving. My thoughts are racing. I feel unstoppable.

What I don't realize is that my eyes are probably bugged out of my head.

Around 2:30 a.m., my general manager walks through the lobby. She lives on property. Sharp. Observant.

She looks at me.

"Gary... you okay?"

"I'm great," I say. Way too fast. Way too cheerful.

She studies me for a second.

"You sure?"

"I'm good."

She leaves.

Somehow, I finish the shift. Somehow, I drive home. I tell my wife everything.

She is not amused.

"What were you thinking?"

I drink orange juice. I don't know why.

That's when it hits again, hard.

I'm pacing. Wired. Looping. My wife is furious and scared at the same time.

"Why are you taking drugs?" she asks.

I don't have a good answer.

That was my first experience with MDMA.

Years later, different life, different choices, I'd sell it. Pharmaceutical-grade. Ravers. Parties. A chapter I don't glorify and don't erase. It happened.

But that night, working night audit in Kenmore Square while Boston lost its mind, that was the moment I realized how thin the line really is between *doing your job* and *doing something incredibly stupid*.

Hotels put you on that line.

Especially after midnight.

## CHAPTER 12

### Midnight to 3:30 A.M.

There's a specific window during the night audit shift, midnight to 3:30 a.m., where the hotel stops being a business and starts being a filter.

Earlier in the night, things make sense. Business travelers. Delayed flights. Truck drivers. Nurses. Anyone whose profession operates outside normal hours. That's standard. Predictable. Professional.

This window is different.

By this point, the bars are closed. Transportation is thin. People are tired, intoxicated, paranoid, angry, lost, or looking for something they probably shouldn't be looking for. The front desk becomes a checkpoint for everything society doesn't quite know what to do with after midnight.

These are not long stories.

They're fragments.

Encounters.

Questions that shouldn't be questions.

This is what the desk sees between midnight and 3:30 a.m.

## Story One: "Why Are You Watching Me?"

Question: Who usually comes in during these hours?
Answer: The expected ones first. Business travelers. Airline delays. Truckers. Third-shift workers. No issue.

Question: And after that?
Answer: **The rest.**

Homeless.
Drug users.
People drifting because the night ran out of options.

I understand the timing. I don't enjoy it, but I understand it. What always puzzled me were the people who acted like *I* was the problem. I'd be behind the desk, suit, tie, name tag, doing my job. Neutral face. No commentary. No judgment. And yet certain guests would look at me like I was surveilling them.

Africans, in particular, recent arrivals, maybe a year or two in the country. I only note that because of the look: dismissive, suspicious, like I was beneath them somehow.

Which was interesting, considering I controlled the keys.

They'd act as if I was watching them. Tracking them. Interested in what they were doing.

I wasn't.

I don't care what you do.

I care whether you're checking in, checking out, or causing a problem.

That's it.

The perception, though, that I was some kind of observer, was entirely in their head.

## NO VACANCY FOR COMMON SENSE

### Story Two: "Is the Government Going to Call Me?"

Late night. A couple from China. One night stay.

The woman was clearly in charge. Dominant personality. Controlled the interaction. Standard registration card, ID, signature, phone number.

She froze at the phone number.

She looked at me and said, very seriously:

"Is the government going to call me?"

I paused.

Which government?

Ours. The United States government.

No.

They're not calling you. I promise you, nobody here has the time, interest, or budget to call you. You're staying one night. One.

She translated something urgently to the man with her. Whispering. Tapping her phone. Looking at me like I was lying.

"I don't think I should give this," she said.

Fine.

I crossed out the phone number line.

"No phone number needed. Just sign at the bottom."

Now she was concerned about *what she was signing*.

It's a liability acknowledgment. No smoking. No destruction. If you damage the room, you pay. That's it. Every hotel. Everywhere.

She stared at the paper like it was a confession.

At that point, I stopped explaining. Midnight rules apply.

Sign.

Take the keys.

Go to your room.

The moment I removed the phone number, all tension disappeared. Crisis solved.

Which told me everything I needed to know.

### Story Three: "Call the Cops"

This one's more humorous, at least in hindsight.

I'm originally from California. And if you've ever lived out there, you know one thing:

When law enforcement shows up, **someone is going to jail**.

Lights on. Hands out. Conversation over.

That's just how it is.

So when I moved east and started working night audit in New England, what I saw between midnight and 3:30 a.m. genuinely surprised me.

Cops would bring in DUIs.

Not to jail.

To the hotel.

Car towed. Driver escorted inside.

"Check yourself in. Pay for the room."

I'm standing behind the desk thinking:

Isn't this guy supposed to be in cuffs?

Out here, it was routine.

The explanation was always the same, delivered calmly, professionally, without drama:

"Too much paperwork. I want to go home."

And honestly? I get it.

It keeps the roads safe.

Keeps people out of the system.

Stops one bad decision from turning into a permanent record.

Preventative policing. Quietly effective. No speeches. No theatrics.

The guests would pay. They'd say thank you. They'd go to their rooms.

## NO VACANCY FOR COMMON SENSE

Sometimes the cops would get called for disturbances instead. They'd leave, come back down laughing, high-fiving each other.

I'd ask, "What happened?"

"They settled down."

Settled down?

In California, that sentence doesn't exist.

But here's the key difference with New England cops: They tell you **once**.

If they have to come back?

Now you've got a problem.

Which brings me to the party story.

Young crowd. Drinking. Music blasting. Standard late-night nonsense.

I go up first. Knock on the door.

"Hey guys, you need to keep it down."

"Who the fuck are you?"

I already know who's registered in the room.

That's night audit 101. I ask for that person directly.

Second knock. Same response.

Dismissive. Loud. Disrespectful.

At that point, conversation is over.

I call the police.

They don't knock politely.

They **pound**.

Door opens halfway.

"What the fu—"

Badge appears.

"Oh... shit."

Door swings open.

"Everyone against the wall. Music off. Now."

The tone shifts instantly.

The same people who talked tough to me couldn't even make eye contact with the uniform.

The officer laid it out plainly:

"This gentleman works here. He asked you multiple times. You ignored him. You disrespected him. Now we're here."

A few arrests followed. Underage drinking. Party over.

Could it have gone differently? Sure.
If they'd listened the first time.

I don't care what people do in their rooms.
Party. Drink. Whatever.

Just don't be loud.
Don't be disrespectful.
And don't make me come twice.

Because if it gets to the point where I call the police, you've already failed the easiest part of staying out of trouble: **listening**.

I'm front desk.
I bring towels.
Answer questions.
Fix problems.

I'm not dressed like a thug. I'm in a suit and tie. That's the job. That's the role.

And when you ignore that...

Eventually, someone with a badge explains it for me.

# EPILOGUE

## After the Key Is Returned

At the end of every stay, there is a checkout.

Guests leave. Keys are returned. Rooms are reset. The lobby quiets down, at least for a moment. From the outside, it looks like nothing happened. But behind the desk, everything happened.

That's the part most people never see.

Working the front desk taught me more about people than any classroom ever could. Not because of the drama, the complaints, or the occasional absurdity but because of repetition. Patterns. Behavior under pressure. How people treat others when they're tired, stressed, entitled, confused, or simply passing through.

I learned that most people aren't complicated. They're predictable. Business travelers want efficiency. Families want patience. International guests want clarity. Late-night arrivals want mercy. And everyone, every single person, wants to be seen as reasonable, even when they aren't acting that way.

The job forced me to master restraint. To manage my face. To choose professionalism over impulse. To separate what someone was carrying from what they were throwing at me. That skill didn't just keep me employed, it kept me grounded.

## EPILOGUE

I like this work.
Not because it's glamorous.
Not because it's easy.
But because it's honest.
You show up.
You solve problems.
You communicate clearly.
You don't judge.
You don't overreact.
You operate.

Behind every funny story in this book is a simple truth: the front desk is a mirror. People reveal who they are in small moments, when policies apply to them, when expectations collide with reality, when they don't get exactly what they want.

And the longer you stand there, the more you realize something else: most conflicts aren't about rooms, rates, or rules. They're about control, dignity, and self-management.

This book isn't an attack on guests. It's a record of human behavior in transit. Temporary lives intersecting for a night. Sometimes messy. Sometimes hilarious. Sometimes uncomfortable. Always revealing.

So if you've ever wondered what really happens at the front desk, what's noticed, what's remembered, what's quietly handled, now you know.

Eventually, the shift ends. The desk is handed off. Another agent takes over.

But the lessons stay.

And long after the lobby lights dim, one truth remains:

**There's always availability for respect.**
**Common sense, however, is often fully booked.**